ECHOES FROM AN ARROW PIERCED HEART

ECHOES FROM AN ARROW PIERCED HEART

FAID

ISBN: 978-1-3999-5237-8

Published by Percival Media

for whom the angels name…

CONTENTS

ECHOES FROM AN ARROW PIERCED HEART

DECLARATION OF LOVE

This is my declaration of love.

These words have been screaming out
from my soul to be manifested as such.

And if all the ink in the world
would ever dry up.

I shall use every last drop of my blood
to grant you immortality.

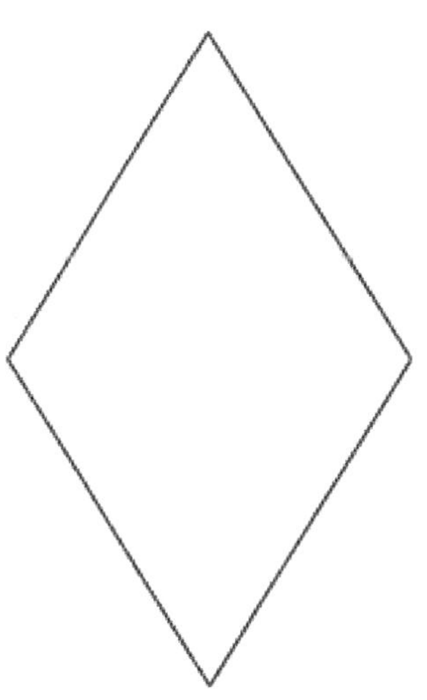

RAISON D'ÊTRE

You are my *raison d'être.*

Every action that I take
is an attempt to serve your divinity.

And if I draw my last breath
without you on my mind

then dying would become
forbidden for me.

DESTINY

There is nothing about you
that I would change.

The entwining of your ancestors
over an eternity

has led to perfection
standing right before me.

How fortunate are my eyes to be functioning
at the same time as your existence?

TRIDENT OF POSEIDON

My love for you is transcendental.

The trident of poseidon
would merely be the size of a fork

if my boundless passion
were to ever manifest.

AMOROUS CADAVER

In death as well as life
my love will remain forevermore.

For when I have perished
and been laid to rest.

The ground above shall tremble

because my heart
will still beat for you.

MATRIMONY PARADISO

With the will of the heavens

the archangel of love
had binded our hearts together.

Impaling my desire for the flesh of another
I had become forever linked to your soul.

A prisoner sentenced for eternity
locked behind the bars of your beauty.

Where not even the angel of death
would be able to free me.

ENCHANTED

I cannot escape from this spell
you have enchanted on my soul.

No distance is far enough
no amount of time would be long enough

and no one could ever come in between us
bounded by diamonds or not.

In this realm and in the afterlife
I will always be chained to your heart.

MY SOLACE

If my legs were severed
I would crawl to you.

If my arms were detached
I would slither to you.

And even if my body
was to be completely annihilated

my spirit would still find
a way to your heart.

For you are my only means of solace.

SWEETNESS

My hunger can no longer be satiated
unless it is fed by your hand.

For the sweetness of honey
has become bland.

Nothing compares
to the taste of your lips.

MEMOIR FROM AN ARROW PIERCED HEART

I still remember the first time I set sights on you
mistakenly thinking you were the prey.

Your piercing eyes like an arrow
shot from the bow of Cupid himself

shattered through my soul
like it were a shield of glass

and conquered my heart
through the gates of my tears.

At that very moment
I had become entirely and eternally yours.

GUIDING LIGHT

You are as inevitable as the moon.

Whichever road I take
you float over my head.

Gifting light to the darkness.

ETERNAL FLAME

My love for you
is that of an eternal flame.

A fire that transcends
the deepest depths of hell.

A tsunami could engulf the whole of the realm
but this blaze would still burn all the same.

SUMMER SKY

My summer sky.
My silent saviour.

Existence would simply be futile
without you watching over me.

The heavens could never compare
to your bountiful beauty.

And when our vessels entwine
we become one with the wind.

Floating in a state of drunken euphoria
denying gravity the ability to ground us.

YEARNING BLOSSOMS

I speak to the flowers
you walk by everyday.

They tell me that they curse at the heavens
for not granting them eyes.

So that they can witness
your beauty in the flesh.

ARISTA

You have harvested a love in me
that could feed mankind for an eternity.

My starving soul was a barren wasteland
before our paths crossed.

But now I have become gluttoned with passion
ever since I have met you

and the remnants of your touch
will continue to provide sustenance to my heart.

Long after you decide to depart.

EYES OF HEAVEN

Your angel eyes leave me blind
to any other sight.

They are gifts from God.

Gazing upon them
grants me a glimpse into heaven.

BLOOD COATED HANDS

My beloved
those innocent hands are coated in blood.

You have gracefully killed any chance
for me to feel this way for anyone else.

My soul is eternally
shackled to yours

with not a key in this world
that could free me from your bind.

I am yours
and you are mine.

DESTINED SOULS

Merely walking past you
rekindles the passion of a lost memory

from when we were lovers
in a past realm.

My desires are resisted against my will
as our eyes meet momentarily.

For the world would be engulfed in flames
if our destined souls were to bind once more.

HIGHER ESSENCE

If I could never feel your essence again
I would sever my hands.

For what use would they be?
The touch of another could never compare.

SERENE SLUMBER

I cannot control the dreams I have
yet you appear in every single one of them.

Residing in my mind all day
providing comfort to my sorrowing heart.

Dancing with my subconsciousness all night
with the moon looming over our souls.

I have never felt more serene
than when we are together in the blissful darkness.

And so my only wish is to sleep forever
so I can live this fantasy for eternity.

BIRTH OF LOVE

Your essence has triggered
the birth of love inside my barren heart.

A place where I felt
none could ever inhabit

is now gracefully wounded
by Cupid's soft dart

bringing life to my cold soul
in the form of your amor.

Where now not even the angel of death
could kill this infinite infatuation.

KOI NO YOKAN

There is not a moment that I could spend
without you in my life anymore.

From the second we crossed paths
your aura had enchanted my vessel

casting a spell
on my unsuspecting heart.

So that I could never love anyone else
the way I long for you.

GOLDEN EVENING

The summer heat of this
golden evening is not enough.

I lie awake trembling
for my heart is still cold.

Only your warm embrace
could put this vessel at ease.

A

You are captured by the arms of another
but your heart belongs to me.

The grip of no mortal
could keep our souls apart.

INCOMPARABLE

If I am never able to see you again
then please take my eyes with you.

Nothing will ever compare to your light
and the sight of anyone else

will only bring pain and misery
upon my longing soul.

GUARDIAN ANGEL

I see your wings
when no one else can.

Purifying the souls
of all those who cross your path.

Beauty that transcends humanity
granting life as well as death.

You have taught me love
saving me from this earth's torment.

Let me reside in your heart indefinitely
so I can be safe for the rest of eternity

my beloved guardian angel.

OASIS

You are an unexpected summer breeze
that has washed away the sunlight of sadness.

I search for your sensation
in everything I see.

Like a bedouin walking through
the sands of the sahara

desperately grasping
at the illusion of your oasis.

FOUNTAIN

I only desire to drink from your fountain
where the elixir of life resides.

My eternal thirst can only be quenched
by the intoxicating sweetness of your taste.

Leaving me in a state of drunken rapture
under the influence of your beauty.

HAVEN

During this warm autumn night
I am stuck in between heaven and hell.

But I met my guardian angel from the east
who brought peace to my nomadic heart.

After my passage around the realm
I had eventually reached my destination.

The sound of the waves
combine with the beat of my heart.

I have finally found my haven
in between your arms.

MANIFESTATION OF PERFECTION

You are the manifestation of perfection.

Even if all the artists in history
were to come to work together

they would never be able to replicate
even just a fraction of your beauty.

Masterpieces like yourself
come once in an eternity.

Only the almighty
can grant justice to your grace.

BITTERSWEET LULLABIES

The shape of your eyes
sing bittersweet lullabies.

Melancholic harmonies
delicately forcing mountains to their knees

spearheading the conquest of my ancestors
well before I was born

to actualise my conception
granting me the purpose

of silencing your pain.

BURNING HOUSE

Another sleepless night
without you by my side.

I am trapped in this burning house
engulfed by my passion I have for you.

And my heart will never be occupied
by love for another ever again.

For you have granted me life
but I want yours to bind with mine.

X

There is no one worthy of my affection
but you and yourself alone.

The world and all its treasure could never tempt me
to fall into the cold embrace of another.

Because when heaven slowly descends into hell
and my pleasure becomes pain.

Only my love for you shall remain
and save me from despair.

BLANKET OF LIGHT

I was dead.

Before the day I was born
I was dead.

And even after then
I was dead.

But you brought me back to life
with your blanket of light.

At that moment of our reunion
when finally I felt a glimpse of your shine.

Eradicating the darkness
that had consumed me

during all those years I loved you
when I was dead.

ROPE OF LOVE

The moment you graced my presence
Cupid had tied my heart to yours.

This rope of love has tethered
our souls for eternity.

And despite this overwhelming bloodlust that I feel
every moment I spend away from you

I do not ever wish for this knot to be loosened
for you are my only reason for existence.

NIRVANA

As I marvel upon your alluring eyes
and our fingertips meet ever so gently.

I am transcendentally teleported back to a time
that could never be perceived by mere mortals.

A past life in which our souls
were entwined in a land of nirvana.

A place that reminds me
of the prison that consumes me.

Every waking moment
that I spend without your touch.

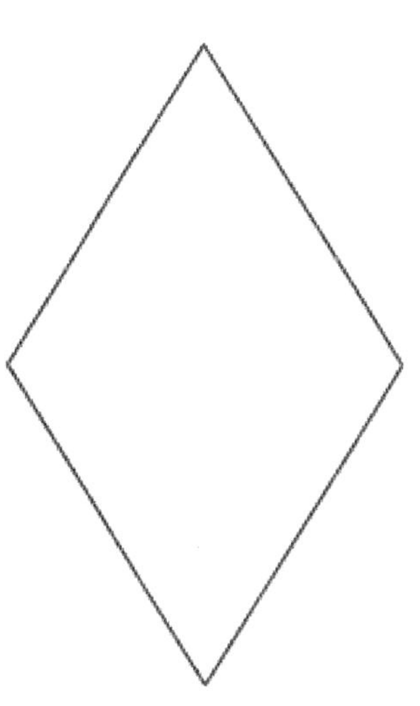

PLEASE DON'T FORGET MY NAME

Please don’t forget my name

when we used to dream
that you would take mine as your own someday

and we would call out for one another
during the exchanging of our essences

intertwining under the crescent
hoping our tranquility remains unscathed.

Please don’t forget my name

when our souls were engraved together with stardust
well before the universe came to be

and with that very dust we were meant
to create immortal stars of the sea.

the secret dream
of the galaxies innate disposition

forming the foundation of the planets

where destiny was fulfilled.

Please don't forget my name

when I cried out for you
with my first ever breath

and your miraculous birth manifested
from the drop of my tears

negating the vow of a tainted blood oath
with the reunion of our longing souls.

Please don't forget my name

when I promised you that death
would become prohibited

if your name is not placed upon my lips
during my very last.

Please don't ever forget my name

because yours will always be etched on my heart.

FORBIDDEN KISS

The taste of your venom
pierces my soul.

You banish me in shame
yet your mouth is ever so comforting.

Do I believe your lips
or the words that come out of them.

ENGEL

I cry out for the name
engraved on my lost heart.

My night-long lament can be heard
by the angels in heaven.

But the one on earth
turns her wings towards me.

I am stranded on this wretched planet
surrounded by a sea of my tears.

Where only you can save me
from drowning in my despair.

I AM NOT THE SAME WHEN YOU ARE NOT AROUND

I am not the same
when you are not around.

Your absence has left
an ever expanding hole within my soul.

That has extended to my outwardly vessel
causing life around me to suffer.

For the world around me
shall know sorrow

and this crime of your departure
shall be paid for by generations of man.

Because until you come back
I will never be the same again.

GOD’S LIGHT

You are perfect in everyway
effortlessly blessing us with God's light.

With your sweet smile
and enchanting eyes.

But greed plagues my heart

and envy grows towards all those
who cross your path.

I want you all to myself
in this life and every other.

SAKURA

Your love is pain
I cannot live with nor without it.

When we are together
and I gaze upon the gates of your tears

the broken remnants of my heart scatter
into the wind like the petals of a cherry blossom.

And whenever we are far apart
my bloom is faced with summers doom

because I crave your essence
like the count himself.

Either way you bring me life
as well as death.

CUSTODIAN OF YOUR PAIN

Your smile speaks to me
without a word needing to be spoken

sheathing the pain
of a thousand deaths.

And if I could I would
relive every single one of them.

To rid you of your suffering.

DYING EMBERS

I frantically run down the path of passion
trying to resurrect the dying embers of your love.

But it works to no avail
your neglect has quenched my very own flame.

From dreaming of intertwining in every lifetime
to wishing our souls were never sewn to begin with.

The occupied side of my bed
feels more empty than ever.

And I can only pray for a bolt of lightning
to reignite our ancient affection.

FALLEN ANGEL

I have become the devil
in your damning departure.

The light in my soul has been devoured
by this intense hatred I have

for all those that came in the way
of our destined love.

And I shall weld my torn heart
with fires from the deepest of hells

so that no one else could ever inhabit
the void you have left.

METAMORPHOSIS

The metamorphosis of earth's mood
I no longer need to weep.

The monsoon rains down tears
cried before moonlight ever shone.

But I question my ache.
Is it the pain of the realm?

Entering through this body
that will eventually outlast my mortality.

Or is it the pain
of my unborn children?

Who were robbed of the chance
to be birthed from her love.

Let me make sense of this pain
so the earth can cry no longer.

AM I NOT DESERVING OF YOUR LOVE?

This heartbreak has equalled
the quaking of earth across continents

killing all remnants of hope
that still resides.

Yet I would still move mountains
to ease your suffering.

Sacrificing my own vessel
to heal your shattered soul.

But it was never enough.
Your sweet love was offered to somebody else.

So I can only hope my pain
was not felt in vain.

And that you will live in eternal bliss
despite my absence.

GHOST OF MY PAST

I long to feel your affection
for just one last time.

My hollow heart has been
looted of all happiness

by the ghost of my past
where you once still loved me.

CRY

The sound of your cry
fills me with a berserking rage.

I would travel to the depths of hell and back
in order to silence your lament

despite the echoes of my very own wail
falling upon deaf ears.

But I will still call out for the name
bearing the unfulfilled soul.

So that destiny might align
in the form of another.

KISS OF LIFE

Your love is of a higher need to me
than oxygen itself.

Like a man drowning
in the darkest depths of the ocean

I am sunken in misery
without your affection.

For you are the key to my heart
that unlocks the blood to flow through my veins

and I would simply be a corpse washed ashore
if it were not for your kiss of life.

SHAPE OF YOU

My sempiternal saviour no more.

The torment of your absence
bestowed upon me

fragmenting my spirit
into a thousand pieces

leaving me to seek refuge
in the embrace of another.

But I refuse their solace
incomparable to your comfort.

For my heart's puzzle
can only be completed

by the shape of you.

ANTIDOTE

You are the antidote
for my shattered heart

yet you appear
in its scattered reflection.

SLEEPING LOVERS

The remnants of your grace
lie deep within my subconscious.

Dancing eternally like predestined lovers
transcending every timeline.

A bond so strong I thought
death would never dare to unbind.

Upon waking nothing besides remains.
I am accompanied by the cold side of my casket.

Inhabited by the void you have left.
When you promised we'd be sleeping lovers

in this life and the next.

SECOND COMING OF YOUR LOVE

You will never know the extent of my pain
and I would like to keep it that way.

For your beauty does not deserve to lie
in the abyss where my despair resides.

But the memories of your voice
is the only vice that keeps me afloat

albeit slowly fading
day by day.

Turning my heart into stone with its blood
no longer coursing through my veins.

But I shall wait patiently
for the second coming of your love.

To finally resurrect my sorrow filled soul
and grant me the paradise of your affection.

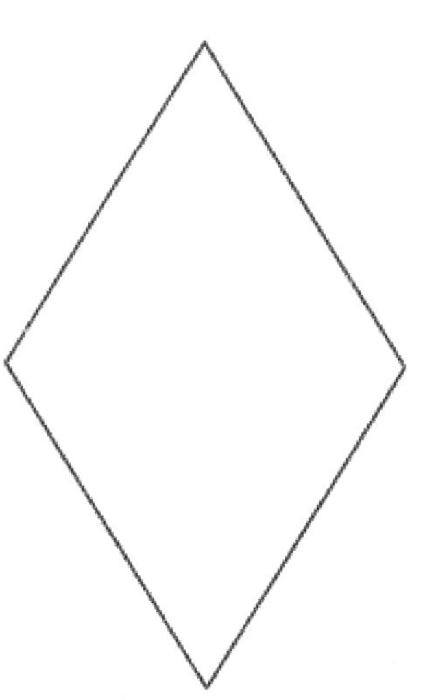

Thank you to the $\overline{IX}CMXCIX$.

Made in the USA
Las Vegas, NV
07 August 2023

75756577R00049